This essay is intended as a short introduction to Dada and Surrealism, not as a guide to the exhibition nor specifically a commentary on the accompanying plates

Most art movements have held their members together through a common visual ideal or idea. The Impressionists or Fauvists have a generic similarity in their work however far the individual painters may vary temperamentally. In Dada and Surrealism, on the other hand, there is an extraordinary variety in the appearance of the works. The unifying factor lies, for Surrealism in particular, in the beliefs and ideas of a group dominated by writers rather than painters, whose chosen field of 'intervention' included not only poetry and art but psychology, philosophy, politics, anthropology and sociology. Indeed to enumerate the fields of interest is to suggest too much a compartmented action, while Surrealism intended to change the whole of life. Artists joined Dada and were welcomed into Surrealism not because they conformed to a particular visual convention but because they shared a state of mind.

Dada and Surrealism differ essentially in that Dada was a continuous attack not just on existing art and society but on itself too ('the true dadaist is against dada'), and maintained a pathological horror of defined beliefs: 'I write a manifesto and I want nothing, yet I say certain things, and in principle I am against manifestoes, as I am also against principles' as Tristan Tzara said in his 'Dada Manifesto' 1918, while Surrealism on the contrary erected a set of strong and even rigid principles. Two years before Dada was officially founded, Marcel Duchamp in Paris in 1914 chose an ordinary manufactured object and signed it, thus creating his first ready-made, the bottlerack. He later said that it was an exercise in the avoidance of taste, an attempt to find an object which left him in a state of indifference, producing a 'visual anaesthesia'. This first attack on the basic principles of aesthetic choice culminated in such dada statements as Ribemont-Dessaignes' 'What is beautiful? what is ugly? what is great, strong, weak? . . . Don't know. What am I? Don't know. Don't know, don't know, don't know.' In 1934, by contrast, André Breton, the founder of Surrealism, wrote 'La Beauté sera convulsive', in which he defined certain constant principles of surrealist beauty in objects, beings or works of art.

But both Dada and Surrealism have roots which go back to Paris before the war. Duchamp was a major influence on both Dada and Surrealism in his ready-mades and in those paintings culminating in *The Bride stripped bare by her bachelors, even*. Their sexual-mechanical analogies were developed by Picabia in his machine paintings, which were among the most striking visual dada works. Jarry and Apollinaire also helped to create an atmosphere which nourished Dada. Jarry's derisive and mocking humour, in works like *Ubu Roi* (first performed in 1896), and his alternative systems of scientific investigation, 'pataphysics', are clear precursors of Dada and later of Surrealism; Apollinaire, who was a close friend of Picabia, Duchamp, Picasso, and de Chirico, was one of the first to value the magic of the commonplace. He introduced scraps of phrases overheard in the street into his poems, and invented the calligramme, the picture-poem which was to influence, among others, Miró. Champion of Cubism, Apollinaire also, before he died in 1918, invented the word 'surrealism' and the concept of the unexpected, of surprise, as the most important ingredient of the new art.

Between 1915 and 1917 in New York, Duchamp and Picabia engaged in an independent proto-dada activity. Duchamp exhibited two ready-mades in 1916 for the first time, and Picabia published in *291* a series of machine portraits deliberately devoid of traditional artistic qualities and imitating as closely as possible mechanical diagrams. In 1917 Duchamp created a scandal by sending in to the first Independents exhibition in New York a porcelain urinal signed R. Mutt, which was 'suppressed' by the hanging committee, although the principle of the exhibition was that anyone paying the entrance fee should have the right to exhibit. Himself a member of the jury, he resigned and published in the second issue of *The Blind Man* a justification of the urinal (*Fountain*) claiming that his purpose was among other things to create a 'new thought' for an object, and that it could not be indecent because such objects were on show everywhere in plumbers' shop windows.

In Paris, Jacques Vaché, equally ignorant of the new dada movement, began to exert a powerful influence over Breton, not through his works (Breton later said that it was his fortune to have created nothing) but through his letters and conversation, which were strongly nihilistic and iconoclastic, with a Jarryesque humour: 'So we don't like ART or artists (down with Apollinaire) . . . however since it is necessary to disgorge a little acid or the old lyricism, let it spurt quickly. . .'

Dada was christened in Zurich in 1916, and the name spread quickly to other groups. It reached its climax internationally between 1918 and 1921 in Berlin, Cologne, Paris and New York. Although it had a short life as a movement, it was remarkably disparate in its manifestations and is very slippery when it comes to a definition. This is partly because it was narcissistically obsessed with its own name and with sequences of definitions which were as broad and confusing as possible:

'Dada alone does not smell: it is nothing, nothing, nothing.
It is like your hopes: nothing.
like your paradise: nothing.
like your idols: nothing.
like your politicians: nothing.
like your heroes: nothing.
like your artists: nothing.
like your religions: nothing . . .'
(Picabia *Manifeste Cannibale dada*)

In Zurich, Dada presented itself as a kind of buffoonery: 'What we call Dada is a harlequinade made of nothingness in which all higher questions are involved, a gladiator's gesture, a play with shabby débris, an execution of postured morality and plenitude,' Hugo Ball wrote in his diary, *Flight out of time*.

Dada began as a spontaneous reflex action of disgust against a rotten world to which nonetheless the Dadaists as artists and poets were beholden economically and culturally. Without any system to oppose to the bourgeois and capitalist world where art was a commercial counter and a form of personal cultural justification Dada reacted with a self-destructive violence.

In his diary for June 1916, four months after he had opened the literary nightclub Cabaret Voltaire in Zurich, Hugo Ball wrote 'The ideals of culture and of art as a programme for a variety show – that is our kind of *Candide* against the times. People act as if nothing had happened. The slaughter increases, and they cling to the prestige of European glory. They are trying to make the impossible possible and to pass off the betrayal of man, the exploitation of the body and soul of the people, and all this civilised carnage as a triumph of European intelligence.

. . . They cannot persuade us to enjoy eating the rotten pie of human flesh that they present to us . . . They cannot expect us to confuse the increasingly disastrous apathy and cold-heartedness with heroism. One day they will have to admit that we reacted very politely, even movingly. The most strident pamphlets did not manage to pour enough contempt and scorn on the universally prevalent hypocrisy.'

Artists and writers of various nationalities, exiles from the war, gathered at Ball's Cabaret Voltaire. It was originally a re-creation of pre-war Berlin literary cabarets but with its simultaneous and abstract poetry, 'negro' music and radical art, it had already begun to provoke its audience in a way that Dada elsewhere, in Berlin, Cologne and Paris, was to bring to a fine art. The daily performances welded the participants, Ball, Tristan Tzara and Marcel Janco from Rumania, Hans Arp from Alsace, Richard Huelsenbeck from Germany, into a close group who felt the need for a review. In June the word 'dada' was agreed as a title: 'Dada is "yes, yes" in Rumanian, "rocking horse and hobby horse" in French. For the Germans it is a sign of foolish naïveté, joy in procreation, and preoccupations with the baby carriage.' (Ball, *Flight out of time*).

Dada in Zurich relied more on art than it did elsewhere. As Arp wrote, 'While the thunder of the batteries rumbled in the distance we pasted, we recited, we versified, we sang with all our soul. We searched for an elementary art that would we thought save mankind from the furious folly of those times.' Arp's own work moved from a severe and simplified geometric abstraction in paper collages in 1915–16 towards a free and spontaneous play on natural forms which through a series of wood reliefs from 1916, coupled with drawings and woodcuts, laid the basis for the organic and bio-morphic forms of his own later work, and of the surrealist works of for example Miró and Tanguy. Eschewing the traditional medium of oil paint on canvas, Arp worked in paper, cardboard, wood, and later string, and several of his works were embroidered by Sophie Taeuber whose own works in the dada period developed a harmonious geometric simplicity, owing something to Klee.

Dada in Berlin emphatically demanded of the artist a direct involvement with life: 'The highest art will be that which in its conscious content presents the thousand-fold problems of the day, the art which has been visibly shattered by the explosions of last week, which is forever trying to collect its limbs after yesterday's crash,' Huelsenbeck wrote in his first Dada manifesto, after returning in 1917 to a Berlin that was half-starved and facing defeat. Chameleon-like, Dada in Berlin was coloured by the tense and revolutionary political situation, but the Dadaists in Berlin had very uneven political affiliations – George Grosz, John Heartfield and Wieland Herzfelde were all members of the Communist Party, while Hausmann, Richard Huelsenbeck and Johannes Baader created instead a kind of alternative programme which earned them the reputation of dilettantes among the political revolutionaries and of Bolsheviks among the bourgeoisie. The Berlin Dadaists invented the technique of photomontage, using photographs and newspaper cuttings to create satirical works in which the combination of fragmented images begins to signify in a new way.

In Cologne in 1919 Max Ernst and Johannes Baargeld initiated a dada activity which, although their first collaboration was on a political review *Der Ventilator* (banned by the British occupying forces), had more in common with Zurich than Berlin. Arp arrived in Cologne at the end of 1919 or early 1920 and produced wood reliefs made from flotsam and jetsam which are close also to the reliefs Schwitters was constructing in Hanover. Ernst and Baargeld made collages, using prints, wallpapers, old engravings, while Ernst in particular used pages from geological textbooks, photographs of knitting patterns, old engravings and a variety of other forms of ready-printed paper. He described his discovery of collage in 'Inspiration to order':

'In the days when we were most keen on research and most excited by our first discoveries in the realm of *collage*, we would come by chance . . . on the pages of a catalogue containing plates for anatomical or physical demonstration and found that these provided contiguously figurative elements so mutually distant that the very absurdity of their collection produced in us a hallucinating succession of contradictory images . . . These images themselves brought forth a new plane in order to meet in a new unknown (the plane of non-suitability). Thereupon it was enough either by painting or by drawing to add, thereby only obediently reproducing what is visible within us, a colour, a scrawl, a landscape foreign to the objects depicted, the desert, the sky, a geological section, a floor, a single straight line expressing the horizon, and a fixed and faithful image was obtained; what previously had been merely a common-place page of advertising became a drama revealing our most secret desires.' Many of these are not strictly speaking collages at all, but simply transform the original with a few marks of a pencil, to achieve the 'disorientation' of the spectator with either lyrical or disquieting effect.

These collages by Ernst are especially important because in his preface to Ernst's exhibition in Paris in 1921, Breton recognised in them a visual parallel to what he was later to define as the crucial surrealist image: 'It is the marvellous faculty of attaining two widely separate realities without departing from the realm of our experience, and drawing a spark from their contact . . .' The juxtapositions of dissimilar objects in these collages was a direct visual equivalent to the poetic image the Surrealists were to seek in their writing, and whose classic formulation was Lautréamont's 'as beautiful as the chance encounter of the sewing machine and the umbrella on a dissecting table'.

Surrealism was founded as a movement in 1924, when Breton's first *Manifesto of Surrealism* was published, the review *La Revolution Surréaliste* was founded, and a 'Bureau of surrealist research' was established. Breton traced the beginning of Surrealism back to the automatic texts he and Soupault had published in their review *Littérature* in 1919. Between 1922 and 1924 the future surrealist group had experimented with explorations of the unconscious through 'hypnotic sleeps' – a technique of self-induced trances borrowed from mediums – as well as dreams. Dada had been a necessary interlude, in 1920 and 1921, but its tyranny of chaos was finally unacceptable to this group who wished to replace it with something positive, though equally subversive.

The definition of Surrealism in the first *Manifesto* was intended to be definitive and was set out like encyclopaedia entries:

'SURREALISM, n.m. Pure psychic automatism by which it is intended to express, either verbally or in writing, the true working of thought. Thought dictated in the absence of all control exerted by reason, and outside all aesthetic or moral pre-occupations.

Encycl. philos. Surrealism is based on the belief in the superior reality of certain forms of association heretofore neglected, in the omnipotence of the dream, and in the disinterested play of thought. It leads to the permanent destruction of all other psychic mechanisms, and to its substitution for them in the solution of the principal problems of life'.

Although Breton later described the foundation of Surrealism as primarily an attack on a debased language in the interests of poetry, he understood by this an entire way of life, a habit of *disponibilité* which could only be reached by breaking the chains of rationalism. He pays homage to Freud for revealing the importance of the dream's relationship with the unconscious and for restoring its rights to the imagination. He also relates automatic writing to Freud's technique of obtaining as unfettered a monologue as possible from his patients, and barely refers to the influence of the mediums, although he always remained interested in them.

Painting was mentioned only in a footnote in the manifesto, but because Surrealism was to cover all fields of activity, and because so many painters were members of the movement, it was soon to become not only an important theoretical problem but also the form of surrealist expression most publicly accessible. Surrealism had already inherited a number of artists from Dada – Arp, Ernst and Man Ray, for example, and soon gathered others like Miró, Masson, Tanguy, Magritte, attracted to Surrealism because it offered a new imaginative freedom opposed to the formal concerns of Cubism, and a constant and stimulating ferment of new ideas. Surrealism was never static, and the early years of its existence gain much of their extraordinary tension from the differences between its members. Artaud, for example, tried to lead it towards 'the wilder shores of Eastern mysticism'. *La Révolution Surréaliste*, like all subsequent surrealist reviews, turned its attention to politics and psychology, besides the accounts of dreams, and the automatic writing (*textes surréalistes*) which make up a major part of the first issues; it also ran an enquiry on suicide, and reprinted all the newspaper accounts of recent suicides.

There was a lively debate in the early months of Surrealism as to whether there could be surrealist painting. The artist's reliance on conscious learned skills and traditional techniques ruled it out for certain Surrealists such a Pierre Naville, who claimed that there was no such thing as surrealist painting. Breton immediately took up the challenge on behalf of the painters, and wrote a series of articles under the heading 'Surrealism and painting', in which he claims image-making as a no less basic activity than speech, and by then discussing individually a number of painters implies that surrealist painting already exists. As early as 1921, in his preface to Ernst's collages, he had written that 'a landscape into which nothing earthly enters is beyond the reach of our imagination', and now he emphasises the 'window' quality of a painting again, but says that this window must open onto a mental landscape, an interior world.

Breton discusses first the works of two painters who were the major influences on visual Surrealism, and whose works he claims unhesitatingly as surrealist: Picasso, and de Chirico (although he expressed reservations about de Chirico's work after 1918). In Picasso's Cubism he recognised the possibilities offered by the fragmented anatomies and the limitless metaphorical allusions opened up, of which the simplest was the formal analogy drawn in so many cubist pictures between the body of a woman and a musical instrument. Picasso's cubist paintings are a proof that 'the mind talks stubbornly to us of a future continent, and that everyone has the power to accompany an ever more beautiful Alice into Wonderland'. In de Chirico Breton valued the extraordinary unconscious powers invested in the hallucinatory city-scapes and interiors, invested with all the anxiety of a dream. De Chirico explored the relationships between metaphysics and perspective, and developed a fascination for mathematics which appears in the diagrams in his pictures.

The first exhibition of surrealist painting was held in 1925 at the Galerie Pierre, with works by Arp, de Chirico, Max Ernst, Paul Klee, André Masson, Joan Miró,

Picasso, Man Ray and Pierre Roy, and in addition drawings by Dédé Sunbeam, Kristians Tonny, Robert Desnos and Georges Malkine. It was clear that painting was accepted as an intrinsic part of surrealist activity.

The influence of de Chirico had already been manifest in the 1919–23 works by Ernst, and was subsequently to be a powerful impetus for such painters as Tanguy, Magritte and Dali. But the early years of the movement are marked most strongly, visually, by a search for an equivalent to automatic writing. Masson developed a form of very rapid drawing, in Indian ink, with no preconceived idea of a subject. Forms would gradually emerge from the random lines which he would then develop or leave as simple suggestions. His paintings at the time remained strongly cubist, but he sometimes transferred into them the more flowing forms of the automatic drawings as in *Nus et architecture*. In 1927 he began to apply sand randomly to the surface of the canvas, working up the suggested images subsequently. Max Ernst discovered a more mechanical technique which he named 'frottage', which consisted of placing paper over a textured surface and rubbing it with a soft pencil, whence unexpected images would arise, and the original character of the material being studied: wood, string, leaves, would be lost. Ernst described himself as a 'spectator' at the birth of his works, although the final frottage was always a carefully composed image. He later adapted the technique to oil paintings.

Towards the end of the twenties automatism was temporarily eclipsed in favour of works based on a more illusionistic dream-like style. Magritte came to Paris in 1927, and Dali in 1929; Ernst in 1929 created a 'collage-novel' of old engravings, *La femme 100 têtes*. In 1931 the Surrealists began to explore the object as a catalyst of unconscious desires, first in the 'symbolically functioning object' whose source was Giacometti's *Suspended Ball*, and then in a variety of different 'categories' of objects, including the found-object, and the 'assisted ready-made'. The culmination of this was the Charles Ratton Gallery exhibition of surrealist objects in 1936, where the surrealists collection of primitive works was exhibited beside their own.

La Révolution Surréaliste ended in 1929 with the publication of the *Second Manifesto* by Breton. This affirmed their allegiance to dialectical materialism, although the relationship between the Surrealists and the Communist Party (to which Breton, Eluard and Aragon had belonged since 1927) was very shaky, and also pronounced verdicts on a number of Surrealists who had either left the movement or were henceforth excluded, because of political disagreements or because they were condemned for taking up a 'literary career'. The longest and bitterest attack is on Georges Bataille, never himself a member of the movement, who had united many of the dissident Surrealists, including André Masson, around the review he edited from 1929–30, *Documents*. Symptomatic of the tension and unease during the life of the second surrealist review, *Le Surréalisme au Service de la Révolution* (1930–33), was the relationship between Dali and Louis Aragon, who then stood on opposed wings of the movement. Dali was interested in a purely surrealist activity, in a voyage through his own personal erotic obsessions explored through hallucinations and dreams strongly flavoured by his readings of psychology textbooks. Aragon was taking his commitment to the Communist Party more and more seriously, shared their reservations over Dali's excesses, and finally broke with Breton and Surrealism in 1932 over, ironically, a pamphlet Breton had written to defend Aragon against charges of sedition over a revolutionary poem 'Front Rouge', but which had also contained criticisms of the Communist Party's interference in the right of the individual artists to their own choice of expression. Breton maintained a constant polemic against the notion of proletarian literature or art which he believed to be impossible within a bourgeois society. This was a part of perhaps the longest running political debate within Surrealism, and between Surrealism and other political revolutionaries: was it possible to change man's social condition before you changed his habits of thought, his entire mental attitude? Breton maintained that while they were fully committed to social revolution, it was still imperative 'for the experiments of the inner life to continue, without an external check, even a Marxist one'.

After 1933 the increasing polarisation of surrealist activity was exemplified in the glossy review *Minotaure*, which after *Le Surréalisme au Service de la Révolution* had closed in 1933 became the chief surrealist mouthpiece. Heavily weighted towards the Surrealists literary and artistic activity, *Minotaure* ignored their political life which was manifested separately through pamphlets and leaflets. Although in *Minotaure* there was a flowering of visual Surrealism, there were few notable adherents until the end of the decade. Rich international contacts were however established, and surrealist groups were set up in a number of countries including England, Czechoslovakia, Japan. Towards the end of the decade there was a renewed emphasis on automatism, in the works of Dominguez and Paalen, and Breton noted with approval the waning of Dali's influence in favour of that of Tanguy. Matta joined the group in 1938 and his paintings, with their complex layered space suggesting inner landscapes, were an important influence on a generation of American painters, including Gorky, who joined Surrealism in 1944.

After the fall of France in 1940 many Surrealists found their way to the Americas. Breton reached New York in 1941, and from 1942–44 collaborated on a new surrealist review, *VVV*, in which Indian art and forms of esoteric knowledge play a major role, and mark the direction Surrealism moved in after the war, culminating in Breton's book *L'Art Magique* published in 1957.

When Breton returned to Paris after the war he found it largely hostile to him and sympathetic to a new generation of writers, like Sartre, who accused Surrealism of failing to transcend its members' bourgeois origins, of refusing to recognise the real needs of the class it was aspiring to reach. However, a number of surrealist reviews appeared, and major exhibitions testified to its continuing life. A tendency that had appeared early in Surrealism, of a kind of public adoption of surrealist techniques, particularly visual ones, and which had led Breton in 1929 to call for the 'occultation' of Surrealism, became more and more marked after the war. There was also a dispersal of Surrealism itself, with more or less autonomous groups, notably in Belgium with Magritte.

Breton's dislike of the popularisation of Surrealism might seem paradoxical beside his stress on the universal necessity for a surrealist way of life to change the world. But slogans like 'poetry is made by all, not by one', and the emphasis on automatic techniques in writing and art that because they were not dependent on skill but on the imagination, should ideally be open to all, were really intended for those already within the group. Surrealism, as Dada had, stressed the value of collective action, of all kinds of commonly undertaken activities, perhaps as a counterbalance to the tendency to explore private realms of the unconscious and also as a means of linking poetry and painting, but this was always an internal collective activity. To be a Surrealist it was necessary not just to join the group, but to be an initiate.

The reproductions here include no works in the round. They also exclude works which have frequently been reproduced in colour in publications readily available in this country. However, colour postcards of many other works in the exhibition are available at the bookstall.

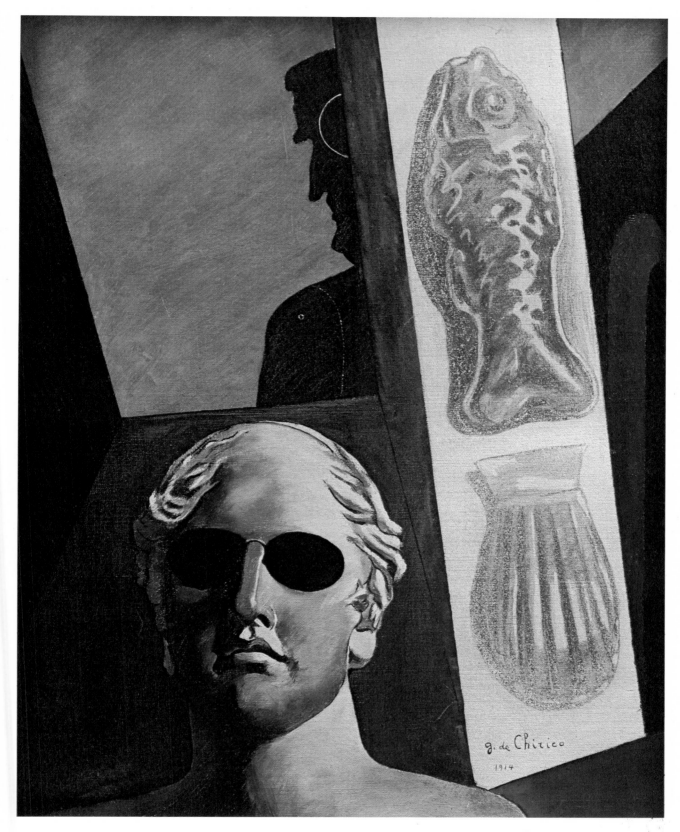

1.9 Giorgio de Chirico, *Portrait of Guillaume Apollinaire*. Musée National d'Art Moderne, Paris

1.10 Giorgio de Chirico, *Gare Montparnasse (Melancholy of departure)*.
1914. James Thrall Soby collection, Connecticut

1.8 Giorgio de Chirico, *Self portrait*. 1913.
The Alex Hillman Family Foundation, New York

1.12 Giorgio de Chirico, *Endless voyage*. 1914.
Wadsworth Atheneum, Hartford, Connecticut

1.14 Giorgio de Chirico, *Melancholy of departure*. 1916. Cofinarte, Switzerland

1.30 Pablo Picasso, *Femme en chemise assise dans un fauteuil*. 1913. Mr and Mrs Victor Ganz

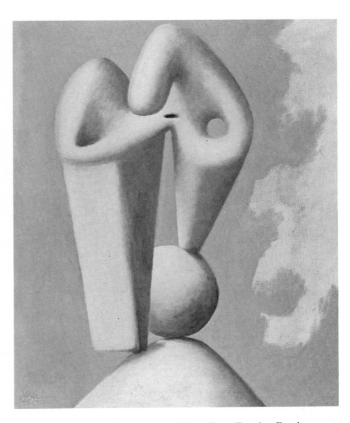

10.8 Pablo Picasso, *Tête: étude pour un monument*. 1929.
Baltimore Museum of Art, gift of the Dexter M. Ferry, Jr,
Trustee Corporation of Detroit, Michigan

10.10 Pablo Picasso, *Femme*. 1930. Galerie Ernst Beyeler, Basel

12.118 Pablo Picasso, *Femme au chapeau assise dans une chaise*. 1938.
Private collection, USA

1.27 Francis Picabia, *Je revois en souvenir ma chère Udnie*. 1914 perhaps begun 1913.
The Museum of Modern Art, New York, Hillman Periodicals Fund 1954

2.41 Francis Picabia, *Voilà la fille née sans mère*. 1916–17. Private collection

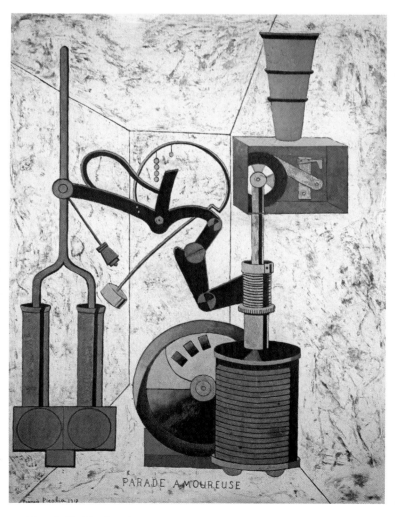

7.7 Francis Picabia, *Parade amoureuse*. 1917.
Mr and Mrs Morton G. Neumann, Chicago

2.25 Man Ray, *Suicide*. 1917. D. and J. Menil collection, Houston

2.3 Jean Crotti, *Crépuscule mécanique*. 1920. Guido Rossi, Milan

2.15 Suzanne Duchamp, *Radiation de deux seuls éloignés*. 1916–20.
Private collection

6.13 Kurt Schwitters, *Mz 439*. 1922 (Relief in blauen Quadrat).
Marlborough Fine Art (London) Ltd

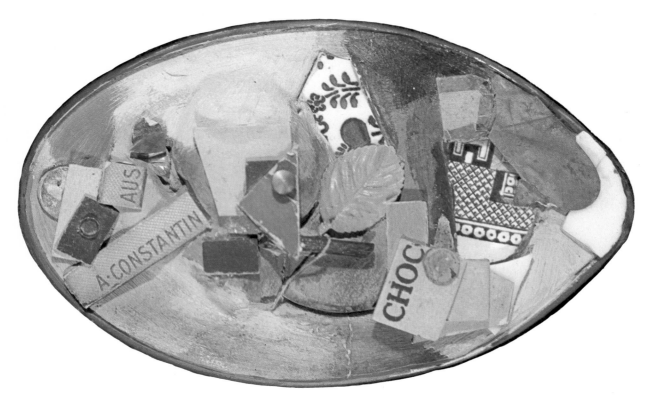

6.10 Kurt Schwitters, *Mirror collage*. 1920. Private collection

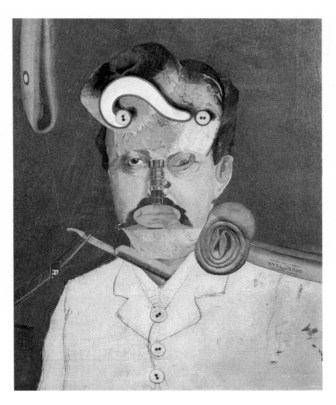

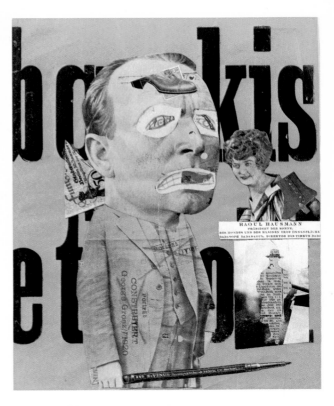

4.27 George Grosz, *Remember Uncle August the unhappy inventor*. 1919. Musée National d'Art Moderne, Paris

4.42 Raoul Hausmann, *The art critic*. 1919–20. Trustees of the Tate Gallery

6.2 Paul Joostens, *Pour Dada*. 1920. Private collection, Milan

8.19 Paul Klee, *Der Orden von Hohen C.* 1921. Private collection

3.11 Jean Arp, *Formes terrestres*. 1917. Private collection

8.3 Jean Arp, *Torse tenant par la bride une tête de cheval*. 1922. Private collection

La puberté proche n'a pas encore enlevé la grâce ténue de nos pléiades/ Le regard de nos yeux pleins d'ombre est dirigé vers le pavé qui va tomber/ La gravitation des ondulations n'existe pas encore

5.27 Max Ernst, *Les Pléiades*. 1920. Private collection

8.14 Max Ernst, *Dans une ville pleine de mystères et . . .* 1923–24. Baron and Baroness J. B. Urvater, Brussels

8.13 Max Ernst, *Sainte Cécile*. 1923. Staatsgalerie, Stuttgart

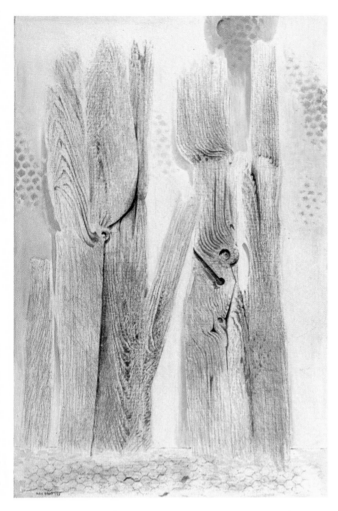

9.15 Max Ernst, *La fôret*. 1925. Galerie Isy Brachot, Brussels

15.10 Max Ernst, *Les phases de la nuit*. 1946. Jeffrey H. Loria collection, New York

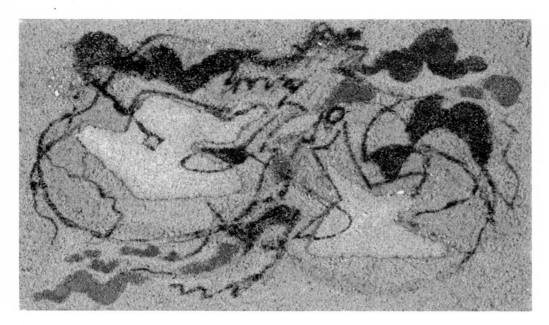

9.47 André Masson, *Deux têtes de mort*. 1926–27. Private collection

9.42 André Masson, *Nus et architecture*. 1924. Selma and Nesuhi Ertegun collection

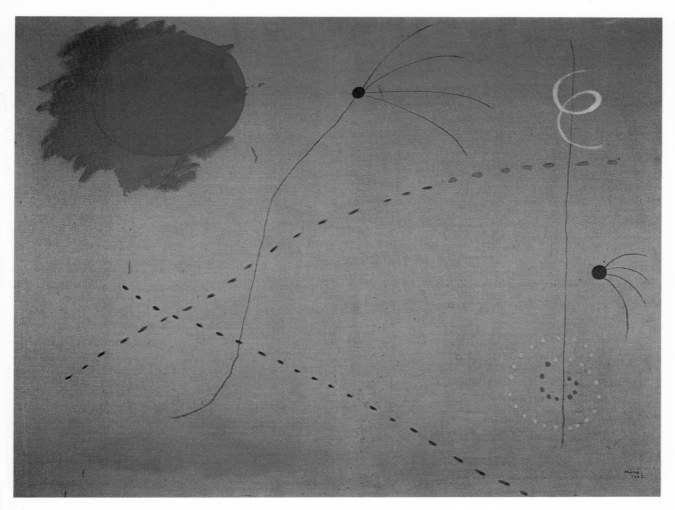

9.53 Joan Miró, *Le cri*. 1925. Private collection

9.58 Joan Miró, '*48*'. 1927. Private collection

10.7 Joan Miró, *Peinture*. 1930. Private collection, USA

9.61 Joan Miró, *La pomme de terre*. 1928. Mr and Mrs Jacques Gelman

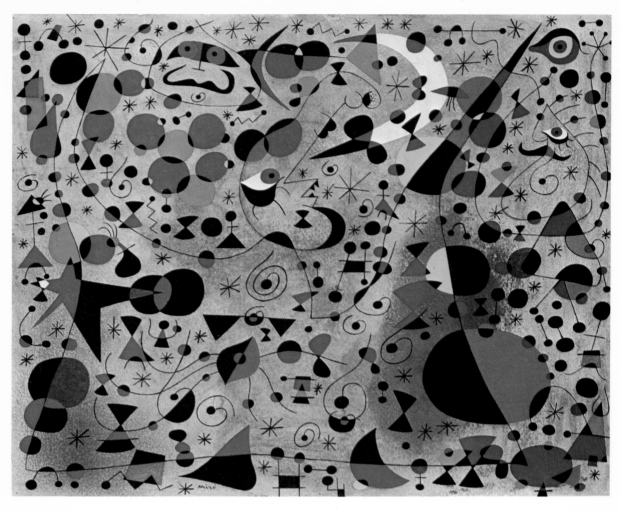

16.23 Joan Miró, *La poétesse*. 1940. Mr and Mrs Ralph Colin, New York

12.97 Joan Miró, *Nature morte avec chaussure*. 1937. James Thrall Soby collection, Connecticut

9.64 Yves Tanguy, *La peur*. 1926. Private collection, New York

9.65 Yves Tanguy, *Il faisait ce qu'il voulait*. 1927.
Richard S. Zeisler, New York

9.66 Yves Tanguy, *Terre d'ombre*. 1927.
Detroit Institute of Arts, gift of Mrs Lydia Winston Malbin 1974

12.124 Yves Tanguy, *Fin de la rampe*. 1934. Private collection

17.40 Yves Tanguy, *Ce matin*. 1951.
Selma and Nesuhi Ertegun collection

12.127 Yves Tanguy, *Ennui et tranquillité*. 1938.
Jeffrey H. Loria collection, New York

9.12 Salvador Dali, *L'énigme du désir*. 1929. Oskar R. Schlag, Zurich

11.9 Salvador Dali, *Gala et l'Angélus de Millet précédant l'arrivée imminente des anamorphoses coniques*. 1933. The National Gallery of Canada, Ottawa

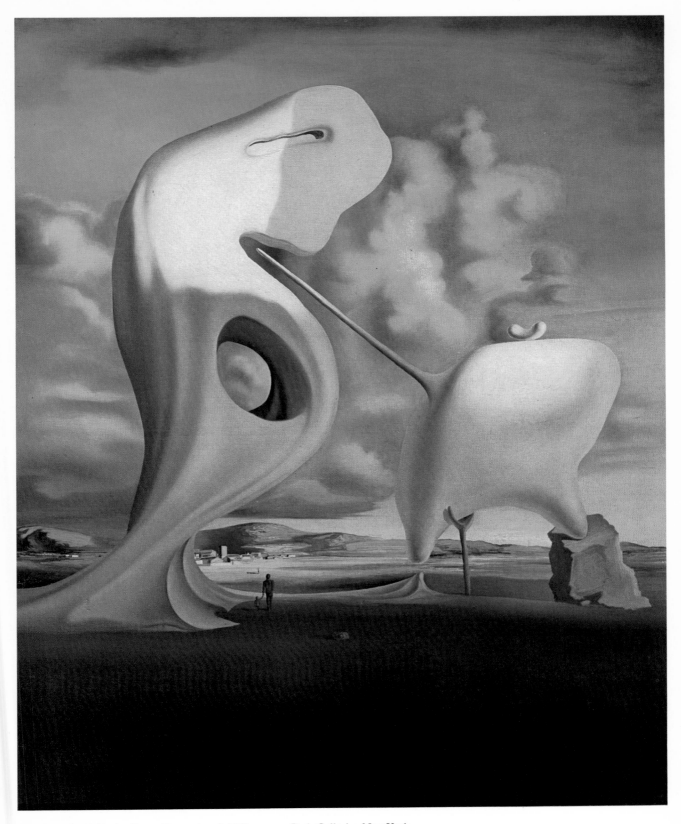

11.8 Salvador Dali, *Angélus architectonique de Millet*. 1933. Perls Galleries, New York

9.30 René Magritte, *Le sens propre*. 1927. Alexander Iolas

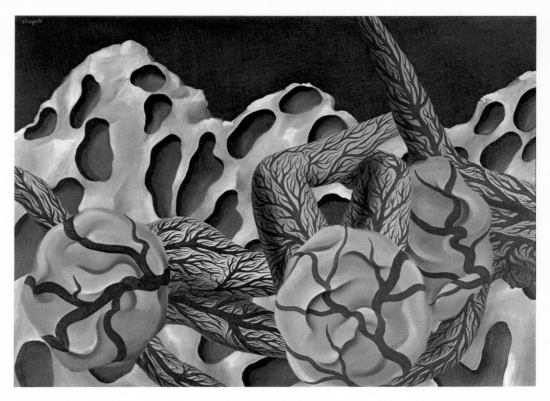

13.7 René Magritte, *Le sang du monde*. 1927. Mme Anne-Marie Gillion Crowet

11.26 René Magritte, *L'attentat*. c.1932. Groenigenmuseum, Brugge

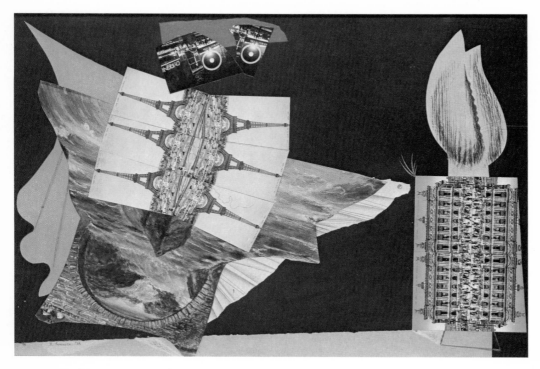

14.46 Roland Penrose, *Magnetic moths*. 1938. Trustees of the Tate Gallery

12.15 Victor Brauner, *Décalcomanie*. 1932. Collection Henriette Gomes

12.23 André Breton, *Objet-poème*. 1937. Private collection

17.11 Joseph Cornell, *Cauda draconis*. 1958. Xavier Fourcade Inc., New York

17.43 Marie Cernisova Toyen, *Château Lacoste*. 1946. Collection Manou Pouderoux, Paris

15.53 Dorothea Tanning, *Eine kleine Nacht Musik*. 1943/44. Private collection

15.35 Matta Echaurren, *Years of fear*. 1942. Solomon R. Guggenheim Museum, New York

12.103 Wolfgang Paalen, *Paysage médusé*. 1937. Lefebvre-Foinet, Paris

15.15 Arshile Gorky, *The sun, the dervish in the tree.* 1944. Joshua Binion Cahn, New York

15.25 Wifredo Lam, *Jungle*. 1944. Private collection

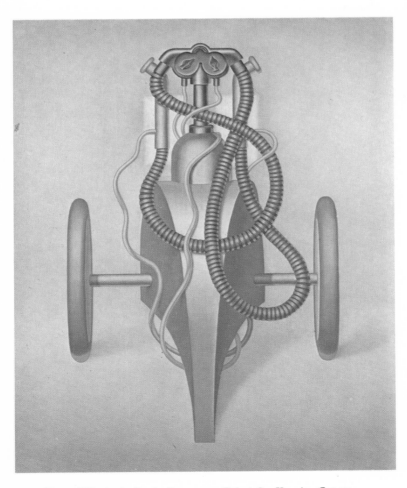

17.19 Konrad Klapheck, *Demi-vièrge*. 1972. Galerie Jan Krugier, Geneva

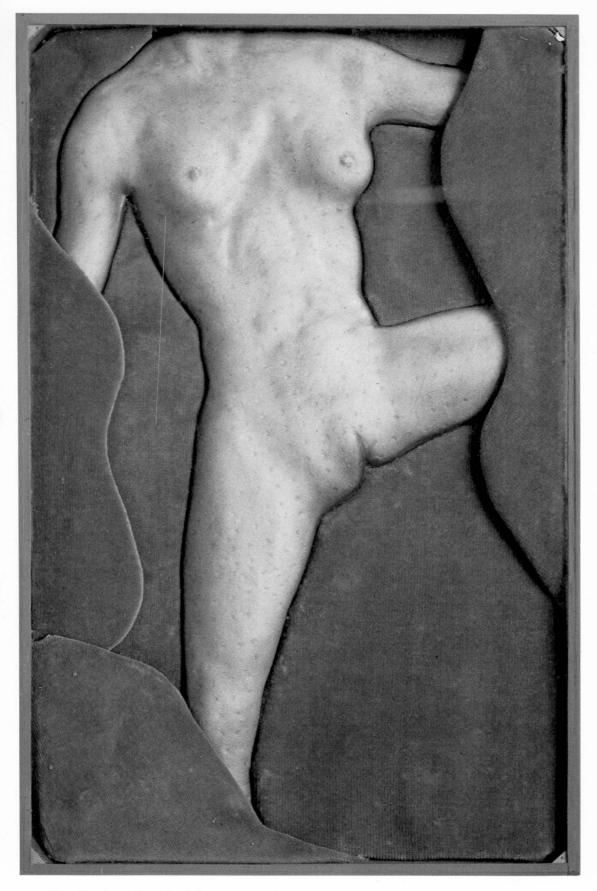

17.12 Marcel Duchamp, *Etant donnés le gaz d'éclairage et la chute d'eau*. 1948–49. Mme Nora Martins Lobo